Contents

Any words appearing in bold, **like this**, are explained in the Glossary

Introduction

Percussion instruments were probably the first musical instruments of all, after the human voice. All percussion instruments produce sound by the impact of one object against another (or, in some cases, by **friction**) and this is the simplest method of producing sound. Percussion is also strongly associated with **rhythm**, and rhythm is central to human life, for example, the rhythms of the heart, breathing, walking, running, chewing food and so on. Some musicians today feel that percussion should not really be thought of as a group of instruments, but as a way of playing. This is partly because the percussion family is so varied, but also because most other types of instrument can also be played using percussive techniques, such as playing bowed stringed instruments *col legno* (tapping the strings with the wooden part of the bow), or rattling the keys of a woodwind instrument (sometimes required in **avant-garde** music).

An extraordinary history

There is no musical culture anywhere in the world that does not have a tradition of making and playing percussion instruments. Virtually every form of classical, popular and folk music in every country involves this family of instruments in some way. Percussion instruments are used in many musical contexts as listed on the next page.

Timpani drums are played in a classical orchestra.

- CLASSICAL MUSIC. Most larger orchestras include a percussion section, which can vary in size.
- BAND AND ENSEMBLE MUSIC. Different types of percussion instruments are used in marching bands, **chamber** groups and even in percussion **ensembles**, where all the instruments used are some form of tuned or untuned percussion.
- POP MUSIC. The drum set began as a theatre instrument (see page 18) but has long since become central to both the sound and the image of popular music. Other forms of percussion are also widely used in popular music. These range from Latin and African drums

The drum set is an instantly recognizable icon of the percussion world.

such as congas, djembes and timbales (see pages 20-21), also used in rock music, to tuned percussion such as the vibraphone.
- FOLK AND WORLD MUSIC. While it is misleading to describe the rest of the world's musical traditions as if they somehow made up a single vast musical **genre**, it is perhaps the only convenient way to begin to examine the vast variety of percussion instruments, such as the drum, used in different cultures worldwide. However, it is interesting to note how many similar designs of percussion instrument, such as the drum, exist all over the world. In that sense, the percussion traditions of different cultures do have a great deal in common.

How percussion instruments are described

Impact

All percussion instruments rely on one object making contact with another in order to produce sound. However, even this is not an ideal definition, as it is also true of many other instruments. A guitar relies on the player's fingers, or a **plectrum** plucking the strings to make a sound. The action of plucking is not normally associated with percussion, but if an electric guitarist plays by 'hammering' the strings against the **frets** with his or her fingertips without plucking the strings, does this somehow transform the guitar into a percussion instrument?

Musicologists have traditionally avoided getting sidetracked into arguments of this kind by using a very precise set of terms to describe how different instruments make sounds. These terms were devised in 1914 by two musicologists, Erich von Hornbostel and Curt Sachs, and have been in use ever since. They deal with every type of instrument, but there are two main categories for percussion instruments. These are:

- MEMBRANOPHONES, which are instruments that rely on an attached vibrating **membrane** to make a sound, including drums of all types
- IDIOPHONES, which are instruments made of materials that produce their sounds directly, without a membrane. This effectively covers every type of percussion instrument other than drums, including

The instruments shown on this page are membranophones.

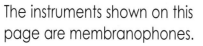

cymbals, bells, gongs, rattles and shakers, woodblocks and tuned percussion such as the xylophone. Within this category, the instruments are then classified according to exactly how the player has to use the instrument to produce a sound, with further categories that describe what the instrument is made of. For example, marimbas and glockenspiels are grouped together because they are both tuned percussion instruments played in a similar way. However, they are then subdivided because the bars of a marimba are made of wood, whereas the bars of a glockenspiel are made of metal.

These instruments above are very different in sound and appearance, but they are all idiophones.

A matter of definition

Despite this careful distinction, there are still grey areas. For example, the **kazoo** has a membrane, but made to vibrate by the player's voice and breath. Log drums, made from hollowed-out trees, are played by beating and can sound very like drums. However, as they have no membrane, log drums are not really drums at all and are therefore not classed as membranophones.

The cajon

The cajon, played in Spain and South America, is a percussion instrument that looks like a wooden box. It has one thin playing surface, which is slapped with the hands. On some models, this can be tightened. Is this a wooden 'membrane'? Or is the cajon an idiophone?

The parts of percussion instruments

Percussion covers many different types of instrument, and any single type of instrument can be designed in a variety of ways. However, all percussion instruments have three important parts, which can be identified on any instrument in the percussion family.

A three-part invention

Every percussion instrument has a surface for striking, a part or area which makes the sound **audible** and/or 'shapes' the sound in the desired way, and one or more parts which allow the sound of the instrument to be changed in some way. Sometimes one part will have two or all three functions. Here are four examples:

- On a DRUM, the surface to be struck is the drumhead (**head**). While this itself makes an audible sound, the sound is then given a **resonant tone** by the shell of the drum. The sound on many drums can be changed by raising the **pitch** of the drumhead by some sort of **tensioning** mechanism. Modern **Western** drums use a series of screw bolts, called tension rods, which fit through holes on a rim that is placed over the edge of the drumhead. The tension rods are then screwed into metal blocks called lugs, which are fixed to the shell. These are then tightened, so raising the tension of the drumhead.

There are three important parts of a Marimba: the bars, the resonators and the supporting frame.

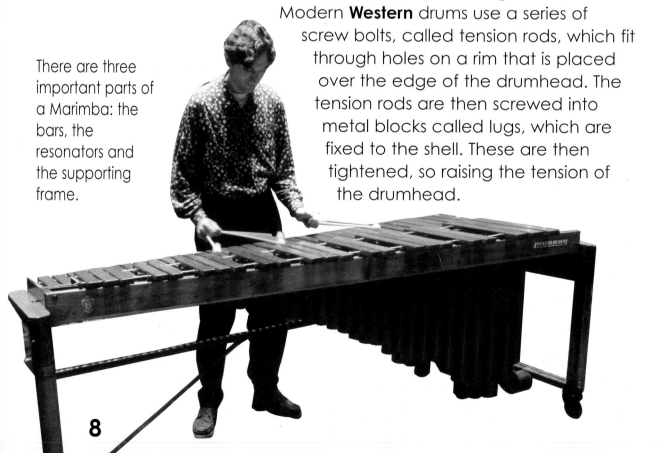

- On a MARIMBA, the surface to be struck is a set of wooden bars. Because the marimba is a tuned percussion instrument, the sound is changed simply by striking different bars. This sound is audible as it is, but is amplified by a set of tube-shaped **resonators**, which hang underneath the instrument.
- On a CYMBAL or TAM-TAM, the striking surface, the area which makes the sound audible and the area which can be used to change the sound – for example, by **damping**, **choking** or adding **sizzlers** – are one and the same.

Can you identify the important parts of these instruments?

- On a MARACA, the striking surface is the inside of the instrument. The sound is made more audible by the hollow area of the instrument. The sound is altered by varying the speed, direction and amount of force used in shaking the instrument, so the mechanism for changing the sound is, essentially, the handle!

Sticks and beaters

Some instruments may seem to be missing one of these elements – but a bit of careful thinking will show that they are always present, even in the design of a very simple instrument, such as a woodblock. It has a striking surface, and a hollowed-out area that creates a sharp, distinct sound. However, how can the sound be changed? The answer is that all percussion instruments require the use of an object to strike them, which is really a part of the instrument itself – a stick or beater, the human hand, or, in the case of bells and shakers, something contained within the instrument. In the case of a woodblock, the sound is simply changed by using a softer or harder beater. This applies to many other percussion instruments, too.

Orchestral and band drums

The various specialized drums that are found in **Western** orchestral and marching band music are quite similar in many ways. This is because both ranges of drums have evolved from various earlier **military** drums.

Standard orchestral drums

Although many types of drum can feature in the percussion sections of Western orchestras, some are specifically associated with this type of music:

The timpani are just one of the types of drum used in orchestral music.

- THE **SNARE** DRUM is a **double-headed** drum with a set of wires stretched across the bottom **head**, producing a buzzing sound when the drum is struck. Drums of this type are also used in popular and marching band music. The orchestral snare drum is of a particular design which is deeper than a rock or jazz snare drum, but shallower than a marching band snare drum. It is sometimes referred to as a 'side drum' because of the playing position of the military drum from which it was developed.

- THE **TENOR** DRUM is also double-headed. It is deeper than the snare drum and has no snare wires. It has a dark, booming **tone**.

- THE **BASS** DRUM is a very large, double-headed drum that can produce a range of sounds from a muffled rumble to a thunderous crack, depending on how hard it is played. The orchestral bass drum is much bigger than the bass drums used as a part of rock and jazz drum sets.

- THE TIMPANI are perhaps the drums most associated with classical music. They were developed from military drums that were played on horseback. They are very large drums with a single head stretched over a metal bowl. Modern timpani can be tuned to a range of notes with pedals that change the **tension** of the head.

Marching band drums

- THE SNARE DRUM used in marching bands is larger and louder than the type used in orchestral music. The player 'wears' the drum, which is slung in front of the body at a slight angle to allow the player to march. This means that the player has to hold one stick pointing inwards while the other points outwards in order to play the drum. Because this technique is traditionally taught to drum students, it is also used by many classical and jazz players, as well as some rock players.

- THE BASS DRUM played by marching band drummers is strapped to the player's chest and is played on both sides. In American marching bands there are often several bass drums tuned to different **pitches**.

- MARCHING TOMS are related to concert toms. These **single-headed**, **melodic** drums are strapped in front of the player. They usually come as a set of several drums of different sizes. Many examples have an angled opening at the bottom, which encourages the sound to project outwards rather downwards.

Marching toms are of a design unique to marching bands.

Cymbals, gongs and bells

These three types of instrument are related, although they actually evolved in very different ways.

Cymbals

Cymbals are used in all kinds of music throughout the world. These instruments have probably been in use for around three thousand years and there is evidence to suggest that they evolved from metal drinking bowls. One well-known example of ancient cymbals was the pair of instruments that

Cymbals are made in a wide range of sizes and thicknesses.

were found buried with the mummified body of the musician Ankhape, who lived in ancient Egypt during the first century BCE. However, the two most important cymbal-making traditions evolved in China and Turkey. Virtually all modern cymbals are based on these designs, which are quite different in sound and appearance. Cymbals are generally made of bronze, which is a mixture of copper and tin. However, other metals can be used, including brass (a mixture of copper and zinc) or nickel-silver (a mixture of nickel and silver).

A cymbal is essentially a disc of metal with a slight downward curve toward the edge and, usually, an upward-curved bell shape in the centre, although a few designs don't have this. There is a hole in the centre, which allows the cymbal to be suspended on a stand or attached to a handle. Chinese cymbals, however, also have an upturned area around the edge. Cymbals can be played in two ways. They can be struck with a stick or beater, or two cymbals can be clashed together. There are different sizes and thicknesses of cymbal, which produce a variety of sounds. They are played on stands in classical and popular music. Classical players will also use a pair of matched cymbals on strap handles that are clashed together. Marching band players can also use a pair of cymbals in this way. A similar effect is produced by an instrument called a hi-hat, used in popular music, which has two cymbals on a stand attached to a pedal. The cymbals are clashed together when the pedal is pressed.

This is one type of gong from Malaysia.

Gongs

Gongs differ from cymbals in that they have no central hole, but are instead suspended from one edge. They are almost always made of bronze and come in a wide range of sizes. The gongs most widely used today are Chinese in origin. Unlike the crash produced by cymbals, gongs have a more subtle and rich sound. They are often referred to by their Chinese names, such as the **onomatopoeic** tam-tam and the descriptively named wind gong, which produces a sustained hissing sound. Gongs are used in classical music, occasionally in rock and, of course, in traditional Chinese music.

Bells

Bells are usually thought of as **spherical** or cup-shaped metal instruments. They may have a suspended internal hammer called a clapper. They are found in many cultures and have been made as small as a pea (tiny Indian bells known as 'cat bells') and as large as a house! They are one of the most widely known types of percussion instrument.

Woodblocks, cowbells and hand percussion

These instruments are quite diverse in terms of how they are made and played. However, they are often found together in certain forms of music, such as classical, Latin American and folk music, so it can be useful to be able to distinguish them when they are seen together.

Woodblocks

Woodblocks are, unsurprisingly, made of hard wood. There are several different types, but the two most common varieties are:

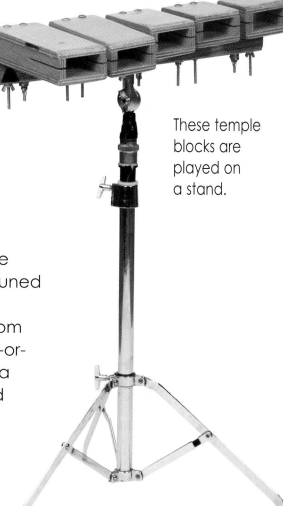

These temple blocks are played on a stand.

- the basic WOODBLOCK, which is shaped like an oblong box with one or more slits cut along its length. It is made in several different sizes, is mounted on a clamp and is played with a stick or beater. It produces a crisp, hard 'clack' sound.
- TEMPLE BLOCKS, which also come in various sizes and are often played on a stand in tuned sets. Of Chinese origin, the traditional design is made from camphor wood and is more-or-less **spherical** in shape, with a hollowed-out interior (this led to their being nicknamed 'skulls' at one time). There are also Western designs that are cube-shaped.

Cowbells

As the name implies, these are similar to the traditional metal bells tied around the necks of cattle. There are several different kinds. There are **chromatically** tuned sets of cowbells, which are usually played by classical percussionists, particularly when playing in percussion **ensemble** pieces. These are very similar in shape to the traditional cattle bell. The sound comes out through the open, wider end. The narrow end is closed and may have a hole or fitting for mounting the instrument on a stand. Some types have no hole and are simply held in the hand, while others have a handle. A hammer handle is sometimes used as a beater for hand-held cowbells.

Latin American cowbells come in several sizes and are usually shaped like a metal box, narrower at one end than the other.

Hand percussion

The phrase 'hand percussion' or auxillary percussion is used by percussionists to describe any small instrument that is held in the hand. Some examples of these include the following:

- The TAMBOURINE is a circular frame with metal jingles attached. Some types also have a **head** attached, like a frame drum.
- MARACAS are traditional Latin American hand-held shakers made from hard leather, wood, metal or plastic and filled with hard pellets or seeds. There are many other types of shaker, such as the tube-shaped chocolo.
- SLEIGH BELLS are a set of small jingling bells attached to a handle; they are widely used in Christmas music.

The tambourine.

Tuned percussion

While many kinds of percussion can be tuned to an extent – for example, the **pitches** of a set of drums can be adjusted to produce a range of notes – the phrase 'tuned percussion' is usually used to describe **melodic** percussion instruments, which play specific notes like a piano. These instruments are laid out in a similar way to a piano keyboard. They will usually consist of a set of bars for striking and will often have tubes suspended beneath the bars to **amplify** the sound of the bars. They are usually used in classical music, but some similar instruments are used in marching bands.

The GLOCKENSPIEL (the name is German and effectively means 'playable bells') is a set of high-pitched metal bars that have a distinctive, bright sound. There are also glockenspiels that have a keyboard mechanism – one type of which is called the **celeste** (which is used in the famous 'Dance of the Sugar-Plum Fairy' by the Russian composer Tchaikovsky (1840–1893) – and a version mounted on a portable frame for use by marching bands. This type is usually known as the **lyre** bells, because the frame looks similar to the frame of a lyre, which is a stringed instrument.

The XYLOPHONE has wooden bars, which give a distinctive 'plink' sound when struck with a hard beater.

The playing technique shown here can be applied to many tuned percussion instruments.

The MARIMBA is essentially a **bass** xylophone. It plays lower notes and has a warmer, more **resonant** tone than the xylophone. There is also an old instrument that can cover the range of the xylophone plus part of the range of the marimba. It is called, reasonably enough, the XYLORIMBA.

The TUBAPHONE is more unusual and consists of a set of tuned metal tubes instead of bars. Like the glockenspiel, there are versions designed for both orchestras and for marching bands.

The VIBRAPHONE is normally associated with jazz, but is also used in some classical pieces such as the opera 'Lulu' by the Austrian composer Alban Berg (1885–1935). It has metal bars and resonating tubes which have small, motor-driven fans at the top. These rotate slowly, adding a shimmering **tremolo** effect to the sound of the bars, which are usually played with soft beaters.

The TUBULAR BELLS, sometimes known as orchestral chimes, are a large, vertical set of bells, which are indeed tubular. They are suspended on a vertical frame and struck near the top with mallets.

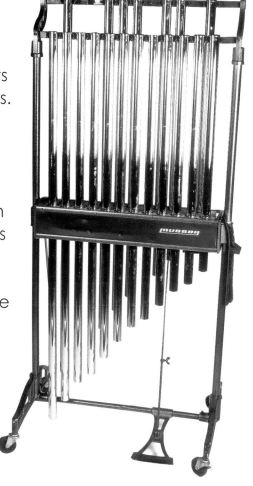

The tubular bells
are a tuned percussion instrument.

ELECTRONIC AND DIGITAL TUNED PERCUSSION

This is a more recent innovation (see the section on electronic drum sets on page 26). They are laid out like other tuned percussion instruments, but each 'bar' consists of a rubbery surface with an electronic sensor underneath. When struck, these bars transmit an electronic signal which the player can adjust in many different ways. This allows the instrument to produce **synthesized** and **sampled** sounds.

Jazz and rock drums

The drum set is one of the most easily recognizable instruments in music. It began as a theatre instrument at a time when theatre bands and orchestras used a set of percussion instruments broadly similar to those used in the symphony orchestra – including a **snare** drum and a **bass** drum. However, the restricted space available in smaller theatres (together with an unwillingness on the part of bandleaders to employ more than one percussionist) would often mean that a single player would play both snare and bass drums. This led to the invention of the bass drum pedal. This device, which remains central to the functioning of the drum set, had a beater attached to a hinged footplate. This made the whole task much easier by allowing the player to use both hands to play the snare drum or other instruments.

A typical drum set

Both jazz and rock drum sets are similar in that each will generally consist of a bass drum, a snare drum, and two or more tom-toms (snare-less drums of varying sizes and **pitches**). Some rock drummers like to use two bass drums and a larger number of tom-toms and even a second, higher-pitched snare drum. The set will also include a number of cymbals, some of which are designed for playing with single, hard strokes ('crash' cymbals), while others are tapped rhythmically in time with the music ('ride'

This is a typical jazz drum set. It includes a bass drum, a snare drum, tom-toms and cymbals.

cymbals), plus a hi-hat, which allows two cymbals to be clashed together with a pedal. The drums and cymbals are played with sticks, brushes (bundles of wire or plastic filaments attached to a handle) or sometimes, for special effects, soft beaters. Some drummers may add other percussion instruments such as

Rock drummers tend to use larger kits.

cowbells or woodblocks (see page 14). Today, the traditional difference between jazz and rock drum sets is one of size. Jazz tends to demand subtler drum sounds and is often played in smaller venues, so jazz sets will often be smaller.

Jazz drums

The use of the drum sets in jazz and popular dance music is virtually as old as the music itself. Early jazz drum sets were often assembled from a variety of different sources, including marching band and **military** instruments. One important innovation was the invention of various devices that allowed the player to clash two cymbals together with a pedal. Together with the bass drum pedal, this enabled the player to play both the 'on-beat' (ONE-two-THREE-four) and the 'off-beat' (one-TWO-three-FOUR) without using hands at all. This eventually evolved into the modern hi-hat.

Rock drums

The growth of rock music placed many new demands on the drum sets. Because of the use of **amplified** instruments and the fact that the music was originally intended to be heard and recognized on the radio, it tended, from the outset, to be louder than jazz. This meant that rock drums, cymbals and stands all became larger, heavier and stronger as the music developed.

Latin and African percussion

The tradition of drumming and percussion playing in these two cultures is very old and still continues to develop, while the playing styles associated with Latin and African music have influenced the rock, pop and jazz music of North America and Europe in many different ways.

A selection of African percussion instruments.

Latin rhythms

The rhythms of Latin and Afro-Cuban music are associated with very specific instruments:

CONGAS are drums that are usually shaped like elongated barrels (traditional congas were in fact made from recycled rum barrel **staves**), although some examples have a **tapered**, cylindrical shape. They have a single **head**, which is played with the hands. Congas can be played singly or in sets of two or more different sizes.

BONGOS are smaller drums of two different sizes. They are usually played as a pair tuned approximately an **octave** apart. They are traditionally held between the player's knees, although more recent bongos have become larger and are often played on a stand, with the player standing or sitting behind them.

TIMBALES are **single-headed** drums with metal shells. They are played with sticks, with the player using both the heads and shells of the drums as striking surfaces.

SMALL PERCUSSION INSTRUMENTS used in Latin music include COWBELLS and MARACAS (see page 15), the GUIRO, which is a ridged tube made from dried **gourd**, metal, wood or **glass-fibre** and played with a scraper, and CLAVES, which are short, smooth wooden sticks that are clicked together, with the player using the cupped palm of one hand as a **resonator**.

African beats

An enormous variety of percussion instruments is used in African music. Interestingly, versions of many of these traditional instruments are now made by **Western** manufacturers using **synthetic** materials.

The DJEMBE is a distinctive single-headed drum with an hour-glass shape which comes in many sizes. It is played with the hands and produces a distinctive range of sounds, ranging from high-**pitched** overtones to deep, booming notes which are made by forcing air through the drum's narrow 'waist' by slapping the head hard in the centre (this technique is also used on the darabouka – see page 22).

The TALKING DRUM is also hour-glass shaped, but it has two heads which are loosely joined together with thin leather **thongs**. It is tucked under the player's arm and is traditionally played with one hand and one stick. When the player squeezes the thongs the drumheads are tightened, raising the pitch of the drum.

The balafon is a type of African xylophone, made from wooden bars with dried gourds underneath, which act as resonators.

21

Middle-Eastern and Far-Eastern percussion

Middle-Eastern percussion instruments

There are several instruments that are used, with some variations in design and name, across many Middle-Eastern and North African countries. Some are also found in nearby parts of Asia and Europe.

The DHUMBEK or DARABOUKA is an hour-glass shaped drum with a single **head**. It is found in several areas including Turkey and the Arab countries. The shell is usually made of metal or pottery. The dhumbek is so named because of the extremely wide range of tones it can produce, from very low (dhum) to very high (BEK!). The low notes are made by slapping the drumhead hard in the centre, forcing air through the narrow 'waist' of the drum, as with the African djembe (see page 21).

The TAR is an Arab frame drum (frame drums have very shallow shells which act as frames for stretching the drumhead rather than acting as **resonators**) with a head made from stretched goatskin. It is played with the hands and fingertips and has a remarkably delicate and **resonant** sound.

The RIQ is the Egyptian equivalent of the tambourine. It is a shallow, round frame drum with a goatskin head and several sets of jingles.

The dhumbek or darabouka is widely used in Middle-Eastern music.

Far-Eastern percussion

Percussion instruments in China and Japan often have religious uses.

TAIKO DRUMS are traditional Japanese drums used in playing *kagura* music (the name means 'God music'). New *kagura* music is still being written today and there are several famous groups of taiko drummers that tour other countries to perform the music.

CHINESE TOM-TOMS are the English name given to traditional Chinese drums with wood shells and two heads made from pigskin. Although mainly associated with Chinese classical music, they were also used in the **West** as parts of the first drum kits, when they were often played to produce 'jungle' sound effects. They are traditionally painted with a bright red lacquer. While the very largest examples produce a deep booming sound, the smaller, shallower sizes produce a gentle, delicate **tone**, particularly if they are played with a soft beater. They have metal rings attached to the shells, which allow them to be suspended from stands.

Japanese taiko drums can reach immense sizes!

CUP GONGS are found in both Japan and China. They are simple looking bronze bowls, which are made in many different sizes. They are rested, open end up, on a cushioned support, and played gently with a wooden beater covered in soft leather. They have a complex yet delicate tone.

Other GONGS, CYMBALS and BELLS (see pages 12–13) are also important in most forms of Far-Eastern music, from popular entertainment to religious music. For example, large gongs can be found hanging in Japanese religious shrines. In Chinese opera, two cymbals are clashed together to emphasize dramatic situations.

Asian and Australasian percussion

Many percussion instruments have evolved in the musical cultures of India, Java, Bali, Australia and other countries in this region. Despite – or perhaps because of – the fact that many of these instruments sound nothing like **Western** percussion instruments, their unique sounds have attracted audiences and enthusiasts worldwide.

Javanese and Balinese percussion

The GAMELAN ORCHESTRA is a traditional percussion **ensemble** found in Bali and Java. The orchestra uses a range of gongs and tuned metal percussion instruments to produce a highly disciplined form of **rhythmic** music consisting of complex sequences of bell-like **tones**. The instruments include the ageng and suwukan, which are individual gongs of low and high **pitch** respectively; the bonang barung and kengong, which are multiple-gong instruments; the saron, slentem, gender and gangsa, which are all types of tuned percussion made with bronze bars played with wooden beaters and hammers. The orchestra also includes various drums, cymbals and xylophones.

The gamelan orchestra has a distinctive and fascinating sound.

Indian percussion

The TABLA are hand drums with an immediately recognizable sound. They consist of two drums. One is usually made of wood and is roughly cylindrical in shape with a high pitch. The other is basin-shaped and usually made of metal, with a low pitch. Both are **single-headed** drums with closed ends. The heads have black circles on them, made from a sticky paste which, when dry, improves the sound of the drums. The drums are played with a variety of complex hand- and finger-strokes, with the player varying the pitch of the lowest drum by pressing on the head while playing. Each type of stroke has a name, and the process of saying these names aloud has evolved into a musical art in its own right: a kind of 'vocal percussion'.

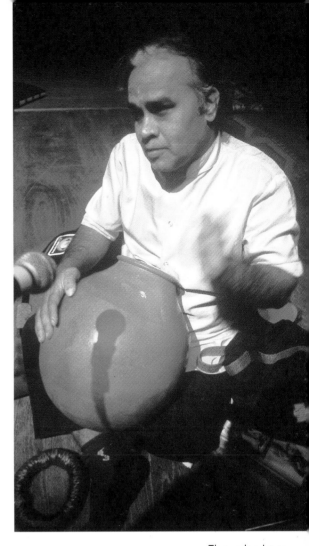

The ghatam can be played both on its own or as part of a musical group.

The GHATAM is a clever instrument, which is essentially a large clay pot with a single hole which is pressed against the player's stomach. The player slaps the ghatam with the left hand to produce low notes while producing higher notes with the fingers and nails of the other hand. By moving the hole closer to and away from the body, the player can produce a variety of tones. This is surprisingly effective – try it (carefully) with a large pottery vase. Indian musicians often say that a large stomach is an advantage for a ghatam player!

Aboriginal Australian percussion

CLAPPERS, PERCUSSION STICKS (which are struck together like claves – see page 21) and STAMPING STICKS (which are beaten upon the ground) are among the percussion instruments used by aboriginal Australians. As with the percussion instruments found in many other cultures, they are strongly associated with religion and ritual.

Percussion and recording/performance technology

Anyone who has heard a drummer practising may wonder why microphones ever need to be used for percussion instruments at all! However, the fact is that microphones have more jobs to do than simply making sounds louder, and both drums and other percussion instruments have to be recorded properly, just like any other instruments.

Drums and live audiences

Drum sets often have microphones placed around them for live rock performances. Volume is one reason for **amplifying** drums. For very large-scale events, such as stadium performances or festivals, the sound of a single unamplified drum sets will not carry very far. This is especially true of outdoor performances, where unamplified sound disappears quickly. In the case of hand drums, such as the conga (see page 20) and djembe (see page 21), or hand percussion such as shakers, the natural sound of the instrument is, in any event, much quieter than a drum set played with sticks, so amplification is essential here too.

They may seem loud enough already, but in performances drums often need amplification.

However, it is also important to mix and shape the sound of all the instruments in a live band, so that the audience hears a pleasing blend of instrumental sounds. Microphones allow the **sound engineer** at the **mixing desk** to produce the best balance of the

A few overhead microphones like this should capture the natural sound of percussion.

various drums and cymbals relative to each other and to the other instruments and voices onstage. The **tone** of the drum sounds can also be altered if need be. One way of doing this is by using microphones clipped to the drums themselves, or other types, which are concealed inside the drum.

Percussion and recording

While it is not usual to amplify classical percussion, when a classical performance is recorded or broadcast these instruments must come through with the necessary definition and balance. It is customary with classical recordings to try to simulate the sound of a concert hall, so the percussion section may be recorded with a few overhead microphones to capture the sound of the section as a whole. Sometimes even this is regarded as intrusive, so the entire recording is made with two microphones for the entire orchestra or **ensemble** – percussion and all.

In the case of rock and pop recordings, the story is very different. In an attempt to get a 'clean', uniform sound, the drums and any percussion instruments may well be recorded with several microphones, often in their own room – or even in a different place altogether. Sometimes parts of the drum set will be recorded first, such as a basic beat on the **snare** and **bass** drums, although this technique is rarely applied to jazz drumming, which relies on a spontaneous performance.

27

Innovative percussion

Perhaps the earliest use of percussion in combination with other technologies was on traditional fairground and cinema organs, where complex mechanical linkages allowed real percussion instruments to be played automatically. Later examples included non-**digital**, electronically produced percussion sounds on some types of electric organ.

However, instrument manufacturers then developed electronic triggers that could be mounted under a drum-like pad. When these were struck, a small electric current could be sent to an electronic 'brain', which in turn generated an appropriate percussion sound. This allowed the production of complete electronic drum sets.

MIDI and sampling

With the invention of **MIDI**, a digital system that allowed many different types of electronic instruments to communicate with each other, it then became possible for electronic drums to produce any number of sounds. This was further improved by a process called **sampling**, which essentially allowed sounds to be digitally recorded, changed in various ways and played back. This was applied to electronic drums, allowing the drummer to play not only drum and percussion sounds but almost any other sound as well.

An electronic drum set gives the drummer access to a much wider range of sounds than a traditional drum set.

Amusingly, one further development was the option to add electronic triggers to ordinary drums. Many drummers found that the sounds their drums made on recordings that had been carefully 'set up' by **sound engineers** (see pages 26–27) were impossible to reproduce during live performances. So they sampled these sounds from their own recordings and then triggered them from their drum set onstage! This is now a widely accepted approach.

Many **DJ**s and musicians incorporate both electronic and traditional percussion into performances.

Drum machines

The invention of the drum machine caused controversy. These inexpensive pieces of equipment began as 'auto-accompaniment' machines, producing pre-set rhythms that could be used to accompany a performance. Later models had improved sounds and could be programmed to produce the exact drum and percussion parts required for a song.

While there was some concern that drum machines would replace 'real' drummers, there has in fact been a resurgence of interest in conventional drums, which are now more popular than ever. Ironically, there are now several 'real' drum sets on the market designed to imitate the sounds of drum machines.

More new ideas

In the meantime, conventional percussion continues to develop. There are now shell-less drums and timpani (designed for ease of transport), African drums made from **synthetic** materials and any number of other new ideas that are constantly being added to the resources available to the modern percussionist.

Glossary

amplify to make louder

audible able to be heard

avant-garde modern, radical and experimental

bass the lowest range of notes in normal use

celeste a keyboard instrument inside which hammers strike small metal plates

chamber old word meaning a room

choking grasping a percussion instrument after striking it to cut off its sound

chromatically using all the notes and half-notes available, rather than the notes of one key

col legno literally 'with wood' – using the stick of a bow to strike the strings of an orchestral stringed instrument

damping muffling the sound of an instrument with the hand or a piece of suitable material

digital using a computer-type 'language' of electronic ones and zeros

DJ from 'disc jockey' – a performer who plays and mixes music from recordings

double-headed a drum with both ends covered with a head (membrane)

ensemble musical performing group which is smaller than an orchestra

frets small strips of metal, wood or gut on the fingerboard of a stringed instrument across which the strings are held when changing notes

friction the force which results when one surface is rubbed against another

genre the type of music – the term can also be applied to other artforms

glass-fibre a substance made from strands of glass mixed with a resin to give a hard material

gourd a type of plant with fruit which becomes hard when hollowed and dried

head the drumhead, usually made of a membrane of skin or synthetic material stretched across the drum

kazoo an instrument containing a membrane which buzzes when the player hums or sings through it

lyre a harp-like stringed instrument with a rectangular frame

melodic relating to melody, or 'tuneful' – when said of a set of drums it means that the drums can play a recognizable series of notes

membrane a thin pliable sheet of material

MIDI musical instrument digital interface – a type of computer language which allows electronic musical instruments to communicate with each other and with computers

military to do with the armed forces

mixing desk a piece of electronic equipment which mixes the sounds from many microphones and/or instruments for a recording or amplified performance

musicologist someone who studies aspects of music other than composition or performance, such as its history and cultural role

octave a sequence of eight whole notes

onomatopoeic a word which evokes the sound made by something – this often applies to percussion instruments, such as the tam-tam

pitch how high or low a note is

plectrum a small hand-held 'plucker' used for playing certain stringed instruments

resonant describes an object or space which vibrates when a sound is made

resonator a resonant component of an instrument designed to reinforce the instrument's sound – it is usually hollow

rhythm the time, pulse and beat of music

rhythmic having a regular beat

sample a short digital sound recording stored in the memory of a computer or electronic instrument

single-headed a drum with only one end closed by a head (membrane)

sizzler a small device such as a loose rivet which can be added to a cymbal to make it produce a sustained hissing sound when struck

snare a set of coiled wires stretched across the underside of a drumhead which adds a buzzing effect to the sound of the drum

sound engineer a person whose job it is to deal with the technical aspects of a recording or amplified performance

spherical shaped like a ball or a globe

staves lengths of wood fixed together to make a barrel

synthesize to create something artificially

synthetic describes something which has been created artificially

tapered gradually becoming thinner or smaller from one end to the other

tenor a medium pitch range which is below alto

tension a sustained and consistent force

thongs small, thin leather straps

tone the quality of a sound made by an instrument, often described in visual terms – bright, dark, rich, thin etc

tremolo an effect caused by rapidly varying the loudness of a note or chord. It is often confused with vibrato, which is a rapid variation in pitch.

West/ern these terms are often used to describe the classical and popular music of Europe and the English-speaking world to distinguish it from the indigenous music of the rest of the world

Index